QUILTS:
The State of an Art

QUILT NATIONAL

Schiffer Publishing Ltd

Box E. Exton, Pennsylvania 19341

ACKNOWLEDGMENTS

Pamela S. Parker, Executive Director, The Dairy Barn
The Dairy Barn Board of Directors
Hilary Fletcher, *Quilt National '85* Coordinator
Randall Fields, *Quilt National '85* Exhibition Designer
Suzy Chesser, Secretary
The Steering Committee: Marvin Fletcher, Claire Gorfinkel, Rosemary Mayronne, Phyllis
    Rovner, Don Taylor, Lujuan Thompson
BEST PRODUCTS FOUNDATION on behalf of BEST PRODUCTS CO. INC.,
    Richmond, Virginia
FAIRFIELD PROCESSING CORPORATION, makers of Poly-fil® Brand Batting,
    Danbury, Connecticut
The Ohio Arts Council
The State of Ohio's Opportunities for the Arts Program
The Athens, Ohio, businesses and organizations that support *Quilt National* and the many
    volunteers who make it possible

COVER: *One Fine Day* by Julie Berner of Eugene, Oregon
BOOK DESIGNER: Chris Brannon
EDITORS: Nancy Roe and Holly Panich
COVER PHOTOGRAPH: Charles H. Merkle
Exhibition Quilts Photographed by BRIAN BLAUSER unless otherwise indicated.

Note: Measurements for the quilts are given with the horizontal dimension first.

QUILTS:
The State of an Art

INTRODUCTION

Quiltmaking's evolution into an art form being explored by more and more artists in both the United States and other countries continues at a rapid pace.

Since *Quilt National '79*, the first juried show of contemporary quilts in the United States, the number of artists submitting works for this pacesetting exhibit has more than doubled. The 1985 biennial drew more than 900 entries from 400 artists representing 44 states, as well as Australia, Switzerland, England, France, Canada, Japan, West Germany and Taiwan.

Many of the artists are painters, printmakers, potters, graphic designers or fiber artists turning to quilts as another medium and, in Linda Karel Sage's phrase, "adding quilting to their working vocabularies." A number of the quiltmakers use paints, dyes and a variety of photographic techniques in their work. Others embellish the surface of their works with beads, ribbons, buttons, embroidery, cut-throughs, applique, ties and the patterning of hand or machine quilting.

For the quilt artist, inspiration can come from almost anything, anywhere: astronomy, mathematics, a Pennsylvania Turnpike tunnel, a California flower-seed farm, a scene painted on a sawblade seen at a county fair, the work of artists such as Matisse, Monet and Diebenkorn. Fabric samples, Japanese kimonos, historical textiles, oriental rugs, a friend's paint rags—all spur creativity.

The artists' descriptions in this catalogue chronicle voyages of self-discovery resulting in highly personal statements. They also give frequent glimpses into the joy and hard work of the creative process. Words such as *exploration, discovery, delight, investigation, evolving* appear again and again. Surprise when a work takes on a life of its own is also recorded, as when Judith Larzelere writes that "a jar or basket form emerged as I worked and unexpectedly dominated the quilt."

Many of the quiltmakers pay homage to their art's roots in the work of anonymous quilters of earlier times, "patterning by women of the past," as Christine Campbell comments. Traditional patterns such as Log Cabin, Quarter Moon, Basket, North Carolina Lily, Coffee Cup, and Pineapple inspire, are incorporated, are "played with" and made new.

All but one of the artists whose work was selected for *Quilt National '85* are women, and works such as Rita DeWitt's "Too Many Airbrushed Smiles," JoAnn Giardano's "Ideal Love Mate Shrines" and Sue Trent's "Corset Quilt" offer comments on women's role in American culture. Many of the works display humor, wit and whimsy as well as social comment.

Over and over, the brief descriptions reveal artists aware of both the world of their art and the larger world and delighting in the pleasure of creation and the opportunity to share their vision. Many echo Ellen Oppenheimer's hope that "those who see this quilt will find delight."

The fourth biennial *Quilt National* documents the growth of a very lively art form and its increasing acceptance by artist and audience. With its bucolic Appalachian setting in an area with a rich tradition of quiltmaking, The Dairy Barn Southeastern Ohio Cultural Arts Center is a perfect foil for the contemporary quilt artists' "celebrations of bold form and vibrant color" and subtle studies of pattern and imagery.

Lloyd E. Herman

JURORS' STATEMENTS

LLOYD E. HERMAN

In the past decade Americans have begun to look at nineteenth century American quilts with new perspectives. We now recognize that their makers—women without formal art training—often embodied sophisticated ideas of composition and coloration not unlike those of twentieth century painters of abstract pictures.

Consequently, both painters and craft artists more familiar with fabric and fiber art techniques have become increasingly interested in the quilt as a medium for their creative expression. *Quilt National* has, more than any other competition in America, both documented this phenomenon and encouraged it. It was a pleasure to serve on the *Quilt National '85* jury and to see the vitality of work in the quilt medium, if "medium" can define an object of three layers stitched together in a sandwich—the upper layer patterned by piecing together bits of cloth and with other embellishments.

"Quilt" as a term has increasingly included a broad range of material and technical possibilities. Machine quilting has replaced hand quilting for many. The traditional use of embroidery on crazy quilts finds new applications on modern quilts, as does the addition of sequins, beads and found objects to their surfaces. Handmade paper and felt, as well as plastic, have found their way into quiltmaking, as have surface images that derive from color copying, photography, various dyeing methods and silkscreening. All have validity in the service of art, but purists might argue that they have no place in the consideration of the quilt.

This year's competition gave its jury an opportunity to consider virtually every possibility explored by quiltmakers today. Preparation of this statement some days after the jurying process limits this juror's recall, but my recollection is primarily of entries employing crisp geometric compositions, often with unorthodox, but pleasing, color and pattern combinations...striped

fabric as a foil for solid colors...careful workmanship of the quilt top, apparently quilted with skill and artistry to enhance its design as it was attached to the other layers...few pictorial quilts that incorporated a fresh or unconventional perspective.

Unfortunately, the popularity of quiltmaking and the number of entries in this competition force a jury to make selections from slides. Though *Quilt National* entrants were requested to submit a detail view along with each full-quilt image, not all did. As a consequence, the jury could not always tell much beyond obvious graphic patterning of entries. Details and descriptions often helped to verify whether quilting techniques, surface embellishments and other details enhanced or detracted from the overall design. But there exists, unfortunately, the possibility that what the jurors could *not* see could seriously flaw the overall success of a quilt design and its execution.

Quilt National offers the chance for quilters to experiment with new material and ideas, but radical departures from the fabric norm either could not be fairly evaluated from their slides, or seemed too distant from the quilt idea to combine well with the majority of entries accepted. Experimental materials and ideas, as well as pictorial quilts, are largely absent from our selection. Our choices do not constitute a survey of all current and valid ideas, but I share the hope of my fellow jurors that our selections will interest those who view them, and provide a glimpse of the vitality of modern quilting.

—Lloyd E. Herman

Lloyd E. Herman has been director of the Renwick gallery in Washington, D.C., since it opened in 1972. A department of the Smithsonian Institution's National Museum of American Art, the Renwick Gallery exhibits the creative accomplishments of American craftsmen

David Hornung

and designers, and selected exhibitions from other countries. Herman has presented more than 80 craft and design exhibitions, and his achievements have won him widespread recognition both in the United States and overseas. He is the author of *American Porcelain: New Expressions in an Ancient Art.*

DAVID HORNUNG

Quiltmakers of the nineteenth century had focused ambitions. They usually aimed to construct a warm bedcover with as much visual wit as could be brought to the salvage of fabric scraps. When a masterpiece of quiltmaking occurred, it was because the craftsmanship or the wit was on a level that transcended the quilt's prosaic purpose. The distinction between the great quilt and the common one was a matter of degree and not kind.

Today the quilt is a multi-leveled artifact which—because of its complex visual form, the materials used and its cultural tradition—is perceived in a cluster of ways, some of them contradictory. To encounter a contemporary quilt hung on a wall in a museum generates in the viewer a kind of confusion not experienced with a painting in a similar context. It is a confusion based on the art form itself and not simply on specifics of content. The question "What is this?" presses itself upon the viewer with as much force as the more desirable "How is this?"

On one level there is the history of the craft to contend with. When we look at a contemporary quilt, we are, to some extent, looking upon a direct reference to the simplicity and integrity of pre-industrial life. But should we literally compare its functionality and design with that of its historical predecessors? Or should we view it as a symbol, an icon that embodies a sense of cultural loss by commemorating the labor of the hand, mind and eye?

On another level, by presenting it on a wall like a painting, we acknowledge the quilt's power as an image. The complex visual language that has always been a part of quiltmaking seems both broad and flexible enough to function in a metaphysical arena.

Today's quiltmakers are far more self-conscious than their ancestors. The complex cultural environment in which they produce their work makes them so. Their individual views on the quilt form itself are as important to their work as any specific decision they might make about color or design. The issues that surround this art form will not go away. Views are diverse; dialogue impassioned.

But despite the range of views and the intensity of argument, there appear to be two discrete categories of activity for the contemporary quiltmaker. The first is to design for use; the second is to design for meaning. Although both employ the same technology and share a common tradition, the distinctions between these activities are radical, and demand two distinct criteria of judgment.

To design for use is a direct extension of historical quiltmaking. Foremost in consideration is the bed or body for which the piece is created. Aspects of form (*e.g.* proportion, material, size, shape and color) should reflect the exigencies of use. It would be appropriate then, to judge this work accordingly—to view it against the backdrop of historic quiltmaking and, by those standards, assess its functionality and craftsmanship as well as its surface embellishments.

To accept the limitations of use is not necessarily as restrictive as it sounds. The great historic quilts were made with the same constraints but still command our admiration and sometimes our awe.

To design for meaning is as much akin to painting and sculpture as it is to the quilt tradition. The physical and visual characteristics of this kind of work are totally subject to the speculation of the artist. All

Terrie Hancock Mangat

aspects of form are variable, attached only to the demands of expression.

This, of course, sounds open and free. But this direction has its constraints too. The restrictions here are imposed by the character of the expression. Artists in any medium who merely 'play' with formal variables run the risk of triviality. The responsibility is for authenticity of vision and a relentless drive toward some notion of truth.

In order for art to be true it must first be authentic. It should, in its every aspect, clearly reflect the hard fought points of definition that gave it being. Everything the quilt is should speak the poetry of the individual who created it.

In addition to authenticity the work should be imbued with poetic insight. The artist's vision, having made itself clear, must then prove interesting. Independence of mind, courage, inventiveness, sensitivity and humanity are qualities that strike the chords of recognition with mystery and inevitability. This is the standard by which works of meaning are judged.

There are those who would question the distinction between functionality and meaning. It has been argued that the quilt form is richer because of the ambiguity of intent that shrouds much contemporary quiltmaking.

This might be true if the two attitudes were not fundamentally contradictory. To do either well, it seems one must be excused from the constraints of the other.

For me, the strongest work in *Quilt National '85* exemplifies the clarity of purpose I advocate. It seems to me that much of this work segregates itself from traditional quiltmaking by an apparent self-consciousness that has long been an aspect of fine art.

To make things even clearer, let's stop calling these objects quilts. Let's call them FABRIC CONSTRUCTIONS.

—*David Hornung*

David Hornung has described himself as "an abstract painter who worked with constructional processes that evolved into quiltmaking." He received the Award of Excellence at *Quilt National '81* and has had numerous one-man shows of his paintings and what he prefers to call "fabric constructions." He is currently teaching at Skidmore College.

TERRIE HANCOCK MANGAT

Quilt National continues to be the proving ground for contemporary quiltmakers. With more than 900 entries from the United States and eight other nations in 1985, the competition has become increasingly more intense and almost mind boggling for the jurors. The overall quality of the slides was good, and since each quilt appears only as good as the slide, the quality of the photography is as important as the quality of the work itself. Participants deny themselves full advantage if they enter only an overall view, since the detail shots tell so much about the actual construction of the work.

In viewing slides of the *Quilt National '85* entries, one becomes aware of the many approaches being taken in quiltmaking. In addition to the traditional formats and techniques, contemporary techniques and variations in construction, materials, and visual content have been added. Of the many important factors in rendering a quilt, the two main considerations are the aesthetic or visual impact and the quality of execution or craftsmanship. The strongest entries evidenced attention to both craftsmanship and visual design.

In our decision making, I felt that we gave precedence to the visual impact of the pieces. Many of the entries were exquisitely crafted but visually ordinary. Others were exciting visually, but with not enough attention paid to the craft and detail of good workmanship. The exceptional pieces were well thought out both visually and in detail of resolution.

I am not a member of the "11 stitches per inch" school. I feel that traditional rules can be stretched and broken or discarded altogether. However, when this is done, attention must be given to developing the work as a unified statement, whatever the materials or techniques used. The maker must substitute his or her own regulations for producing an excellent piece.

As the concepts and boundaries of quiltmaking are being expanded, the burden of more choices faces the maker. The extensive communication and teaching available in quiltmaking today heighten standards and widen possibilities, but they also make it easier for a quiltmaker to fall into the "acceptable formats" and available "tricks of the trade" to produce a nice contemporary quilt. These can be very pleasant pieces, but lack the fire which results in a piece that comes from digging deep within one's self. The new tricks which are available (such as cut-throughs, color xerox, strip-piecing, sew-on embellishments), must be used as means to self-expression along with other techniques, not as ends in themselves. These contemporary techniques are only effective when used with care and totally integrated into the overall work.

The piece by Veronica Fitzgerald that was chosen as Best of Show is a superb example of creative mixed techniques used to express an image strong in design and original in color combinations. The techniques used are so well integrated and secondary to the strong visual image, that it is only on close inspection that one realizes the full extent of the attention to detail. The zigzag feeling of the pieced fabrics is reiterated by the red zigzag machine quilting and further enhanced by the red hand-stitching. With all of the energy and intricate detail going on, one hardly notices the unusual fabric choices exhibited in Fitzgerald's quilt.

Another quilt which overcomes the pitfalls of tricky techniques and traditional patterns is Elaine O'Neil's "Memory Garden." In this work, the overall subtle color and use of pattern pull together a collage of photo images in such a way that both the cyano-type photos and grandma's flower garden pattern become secondary to the overall impact of the piece.

It has been stimulating reviewing such a large collection of work. No doubt many good pieces were not included due to flaws in the jurying system, and I apologize to those artists. It is a difficult task to jury from such overwhelming numbers of slides. I can only hope that each artist with a statement to make will persevere in the pursuit of excellence in expression.

—*Terrie Hancock Mangat*

Terrie Hancock Mangat is an artist who at present works in the medium of quiltmaking. She is a studio artist who does occasional lecturing and workshops in addition to her quiltwork, painting and collage making. Before turning to the quilt medium, Mangat had been a potter and printmaker, with a bachelor's degree in those areas. Her work has been included in all *Quilt National* exhibits, and in 1983 she won the Most Innovative Use of the Medium Award.

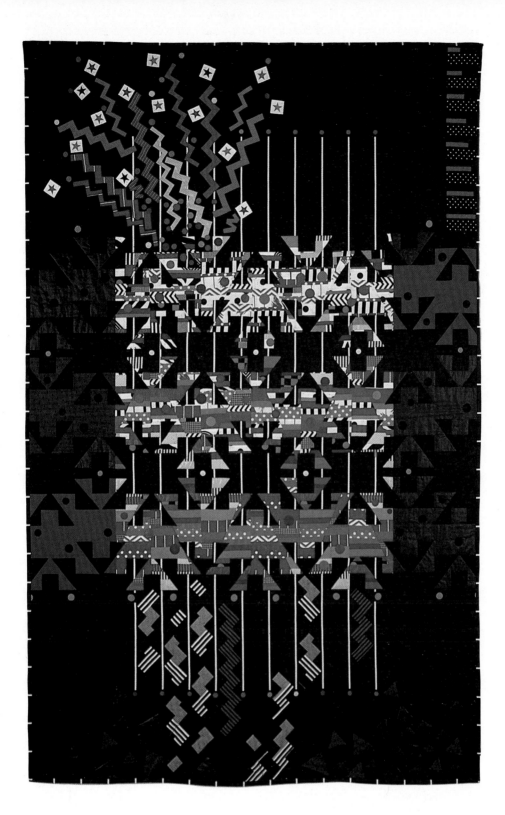

Faye Anderson
Denver, Colorado
Volatile Material
100 percent cotton, polished cotton and cotton batting;
hand applique, reverse applique and strip piecing.
60'' x 93''

Third in a series following "Plane Geometry" and "Solid Geometry," "Trigonometry" was the next logical step. After strip-piecing triangles and assembling them for the background of the three multi-triangled strips, I found my plans altered by the explosive energy that was released in the reverse applique process. I delight in the bright colors and stars reminiscent of sparklers and fireworks; however, the black-on-black applique has, to me, a menacing, Darth Vader-like presence that is an ominous reminder of our precarious existence in an unstable world.

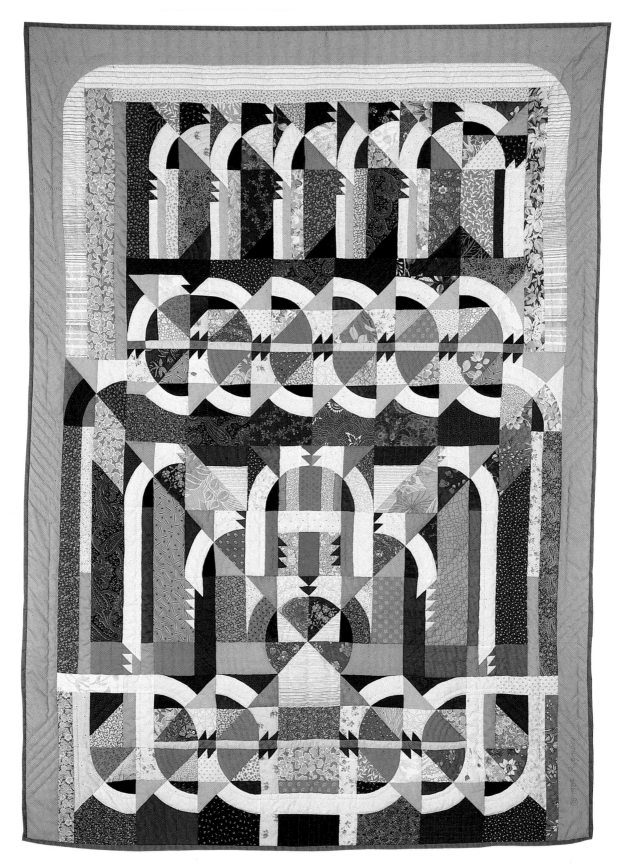

Elaine Plogman
Cincinnati, Ohio
Off to See the Wizard
Cotton and cotton blends; polyester batting; machine
pieced; hand quilted. 53'' x 72''

This quilt is based upon two original blocks in various
arrangements and modifications. Fabric selection was
based upon value rather than color. The major reason
for this piece was that I had recently inherited a fantas-
tic collection of fabric samples from an interior designer
friend and I just had to use them.

Petra Soesemann
Chicago, Illinois
Coffee Cups
Silk, cotton, rayon, synthetic fabrics; polyester batting;
machine pieced and hand appliqued. 75" x 75"

"Coffee Cups" is a visual response to a particularly
kinetic period of time for me: new information, sur-
prising circumstances and unfamiliar situations trigger
energy surges that can be both exhilarating and frantic.

Liz Alpert
Brighton, Massachusetts
The Silent Trooper
100 percent cotton fabric and batting;
hand and machine quilted; hand appliqued. 35" x 51"

Françoise Barnes
Athens, Ohio
Inhibitions 16
Cottons and cotton blends, polyester bat-
ting; machine pieced and hand quilted by
Amish women from Holmes County,
Ohio. 78" x 78"

Invitational

Holley Junker
Sacramento, California
Flowerseed Farm
Pinked and layered cottons and chintz;
machine stitched; hand quilted. 54" x 71"

There is an area in Southern California
where flowers are grown just for their
seeds—miles and miles of pure color.
This place and my wonder at the way
landscapes change and colors blend from
above, come together in this quilt.

**Most Innovative Use of
the Medium Award**
Co-Recipient

Detail

Photo provided by the artist.

Risë Nagin
Pittsburgh, Pennsylvania
Forty-eight Triangles
Silk organza, wool, velvet cotton, polyester, silk, cotton, acetate stained fabrics; acrylic paint; applique, embroidery; layered; pieced. 64¼'' x 42¾''

"Forty-eight Triangles" is a decorative visual game in which one pattern is imposed upon another to form a network of floating triangles on an irregularly patterned ground. It makes references to Art Deco and Japanese fabrics.

Elizabeth Newbill
Mansfield, Ohio
Squaredance
Cotton fabrics; polyester batting; machine pieced; hand quilted by the artist.
50'' x 50''

Although I enjoy a decorative approach in other peoples' work, this does not seem to be a natural direction for me. The dynamics of color contained in simple geometric shapes not only present unlimited possibilities but also seem to most directly express the imagery I seek.

Carol H. Gersen
Exeter, New Hampshire
Thinking of Winter
Machine-pieced cottons, cotton blends, rayons and synthetics; polyester batting; hand quilted. 54" x 54"

As a Californian visiting New Hampshire once accurately observed, New Englanders are obsessed with winter.

Photo provided by the artist.

Yvonne Porcella
Modesto, California
When All the Colors Come Dancing
Cotton fabrics, metallic fabric; cotton polyester batting; hand painted silk lining; hand appliqued; machine pieced; hand quilted. 50" x 72"

Although I enjoy making quilts and pieced clothing, I also find the kimono an exciting art form. The shape is beautiful when displayed, yet the kimono has the added attraction of being wearable. This kimono is larger than life-size—my fantasy that it will be viewed as an art piece.

Invitational

Dinah Prentice
Northampton, England
Hermeneutics
Industrially-dyed calico; calico backed and tied;
machine pieced using original full-sized cartoon as
pattern. 129'' x 90½''

Scratches, dents and marks are not just the written
language. They are those objects that the human mind
imposes intentionality on. Their explicit (sewn) edges,
continually reforming before the eye, now in this
shape, now in that shape, communicate identity and
authority.

Carolyn Accardi
Glens Falls, New York
Untitled # 1
100 percent cotton broadcloth and polished cotton; polyester batting; machine pieced; hand quilted. 84'' x 66''

This particular design was sketched on bristol board and colored with gouache. Once I was satisfied with the color arrangement, I put the design to fabric, matching colors as closely as possible.

Petra Soesemann
Chicago, Illinois
Garden
Silk, cotton, rayon, synthetic fabrics; polyester batting; hand applique; machine pieced and quilted. 78'' x 78''

Pattern functions as an important visual metaphor in all of my work. The mind creates patterns and habits of thought that continually respond, change and evolve. In "Garden," the basic "Quarter Moon" blocks assume different and larger configurations as they are arranged, shifted and rearranged to explore structural possibilities.

Best of Show Award

Photo provided by the artist.

Veronica L. Fitzgerald
LaFollette, Tennessee
Untitled
Machine-pieced and quilted silks and
cottons. 168" x 90"

Quiltmaking is my way of inventing, discovering and solving problems. My eye is
constantly searching for a new way to use
an old pattern; for a more expressive
color combination; for just the right juxtaposition of patterned fabrics; for an
image that speaks. Tedium is interspersed
with joy. Ultimate gratification comes
when I see the finished quilt.

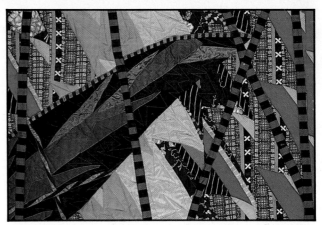

Detail

Carol Keller
Somerville, Massachusetts
Twilight
Hand-dyed cotton and rayon fabrics; strip-pieced by machine; cotton batting; machine quilted. 38" x 43"

In this piece I played with subtle color contrasts to create depth and areas of "transparency" in buildings at the beginning of evening. The quilting stitches are also used to enhance this. This is my first machine-quilted piece, and I love what happens when closely-stitched areas make patches of dense puckers.

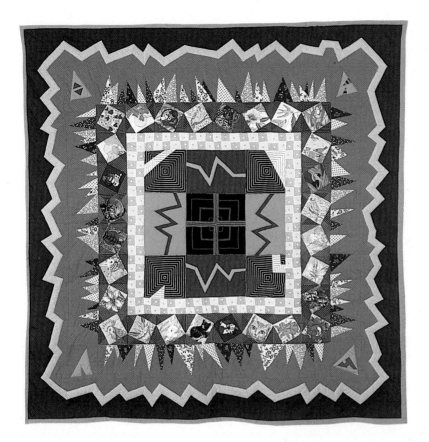

Ellen Oppenheimer
Oakland, California
Zoe's Quilt
Machine-pieced and quilted cotton and blends. 50'' x 50''

This quilt was commissioned to celebrate the birth of a child. As I worked on this quilt I thought about how children learn and relate to their surroundings. I had fun with the colors and images, and I hope that the children both young and old who see this quilt will find delight.

Carol H. Gersen
Exeter, New Hampshire
Bonnema Bedquilt
Machine-pieced top of cottons, cotton-blends and rayons; polyester batting; hand quilted; some fabrics hand painted with procions. 86½'' x 91½''

This quilt was commissioned by my friends Melody and Garrett Bonnema, potters in Western Maine. The palette was selected from Monet's Poplar Series, which has also influenced the Bonnemas' glazing.

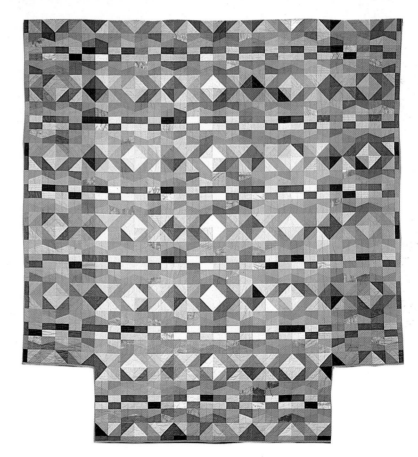

Judy Wasserman Hearst
Milwaukee, Wisconsin
Garden of Indulgent Delight
Hand-appliqued cottons; fabric paint;
polyester batting; machine quilted.
79" x 72"

"Garden of Indulgent Delight" is an
abstract collage. The patterns and colors
of the fabrics inspired the creation of this
quilted fantasy garden.

Photo provided by the artist.

Rebecca Kamm
Decorah, Iowa
Quilted Ocean Park (after Richard Diebenkorn)
Polyester/cotton blend; flannel lined;
hand quilted. 31" x 39"

The bold colors and simple patterns of
Richard Diebenkorn's "Ocean Park"
paintings compelled me to translate one
of them into fabric. The piece is covered
entirely by quilting, and each stitch I
made brought the piece more alive to me.

Photo provided by the artist.

Pauline Burbidge
Nottingham, England
Finn
100 percent cotton fabrics, some hand-dyed; cotton wadding interlining; machine pieced and machine quilted. 93'' x 95''

"Finn" was made in 1983 and is a quilt concerned with flat geometric pattern which portrays an illusion of depth. My source materials were cardboard models of steps together with mirrors, drawings from which provided design ideas for several quilts, including "Finn."
Invitational

Ardyth Davis
Leesburg, Virginia
Tied Bars/Red-Blue
Silk duppioni brushed and sprayed with dyes; pieced; tied with cotton threads; additional dyed elements (bars) applied and tied on. 85'' x 92''

My work in textiles developed from assembling individual elements into large dimensional pieces to using whole pieces of painted cloth, manipulated and tied to create textural fields. My newest work makes use of large panels of painted silk, pieced and tied, with additional elements (bars) tied on.

Ardyth Davis
Leesburg, Virginia
Tied Bars / Mauve-Jade
Silk duppioni brushed with dyes; pieced; tied with
cotton threads; additional dyed and commercial cotton
elements (bars) applied and tied on. 87'' x 92''

My work in textiles developed from assembling individual elements into large dimensional pieces to using
whole pieces of painted cloth manipulated and tied to
create textural fields. My newest work makes use of
large panels of painted silk, pieced and tied, with additional elements (bars) tied on.

Virginia Avery
Port Chester, New York
Leftover Lilies
Design based on "North Carolina Lily"; fabric cotton broadcloth and metallic knit; technique traditional English piecing with paper liners; hand quilted with black thread. 57" x 51"

These are moon-lit lilies drifting on a dark sea, caught here and there with shafts of light from moon and stars. They represent our dreams emerging from consciousness, bathed in light for a little while, then fading out of sight and grasp. The hand quilting carries out the thought, with ever widening circles pierced occasionally by shafts of light.

Invitational

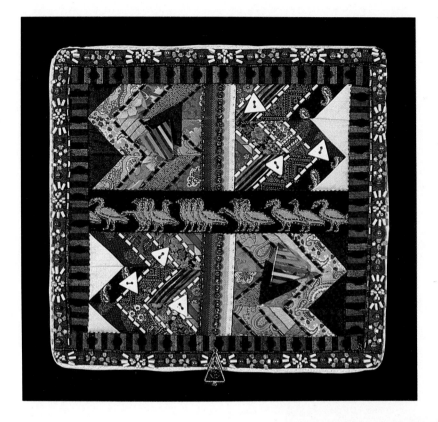

Sally Broadwell
St. Augustine, Florida
Goose Crossing
Fabrics pieced, quilted, beaded, embroidered and embellished. 9¼" x 9"

My work reflects my fascination with historical textiles. The delicacy of Oriental embroideries, the intricacy of Persian rugs, and the opulence of European ecclesiastical vestments have all inspired my contemporary approach to needlework. My technique is a direct evolution of traditional quilting.

Sylvia H. Einstein
Belmont, Massachusetts
Saturday Night in the Park
Machine-pieced cottons and cotton blends; machine quilted with a double needle; hand quilted by Carol Marrochello. 56" x 56"

As a quiltmaker, I am intrigued by the juxtaposition of diversely pattened fabrics and the resulting dialogue they create with color and shape. I try to transcend the seamline while maintaining a subtle grid.

Alex Fuhr
Oxford, Ohio
Untitled
Fiber reactive dye on rayon challis and on cotton broadcloth inner piece; machine pieced; hand hemmed and hand quilted by Alex and Twila Fuhr. 68" x 86"

Donna J. Katz
Evanston, Illinois
Flower Bed
Hand-painted fabric (acrylic on muslin); cotton/polyester; machine pieced; machine quilted. 54" x 54"

Quiltmaking involves piecing together different elements to create a whole. This quilt combines traditional quiltmaking with painting techniques, dissolving the artificial distinctions between art and craft. "Flower Bed" brings to mind a stained glass window. Humorously, the spunky yellow tulip dares to show its face in a tranquil iris world.

Françoise Barnes
Athens, Ohio
S.A.M.Y.
Machine-pieced cottons and cotton blends; polyester batting; hand quilted by Mrs. Leroy Kline. 65'' x 63''

Invitational

People have been waiting to see the monumental influence on my work of my visit to Africa, expecting some drastic changes, I suppose. "Ah," viewers will say, "all this blue must reflect the intense African sky!" The truth is that I only saw washed-out pale blue skies during my stay. No, this quilt has only a little of Africa, some Hundertwasser, a dash of Japan and a lot of S.A.M.Y!

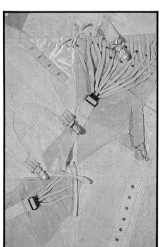

Detail

Sue Trent
Hattiesburg, Mississippi
Corset Quilt
Crazy quilt of corsets and girdles is pieced and sewn together by machine; tufted with pink ties; quilted by machine.
75½'' x 90½''

My works focus on images of women and images of who we are as American people. While my cloth constructions are often but not always in the form of quilts, they always combine women's traditional methods of fabric construction and decoration with critical perspectives on the American identity.

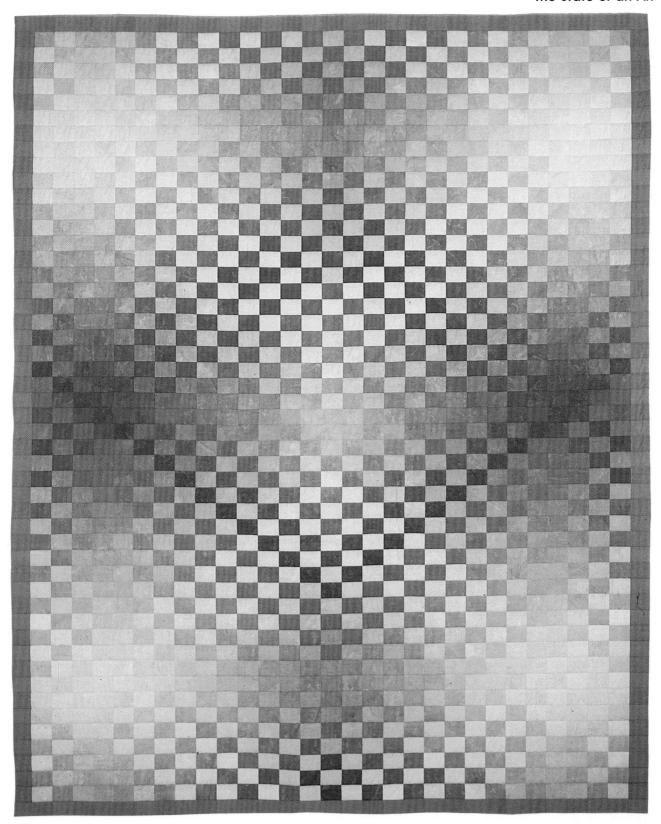

Jan Myers
Minneapolis, Minnesota
Galaxial Four-Patch
Hand-dyed cotton muslin; machine pieced by Joanne
Olson; machine quilted. 63'' x 74''

Invitational

"Galaxial Four-Patch" is a very formal piece in a long
series of "grid works" exploring color and light relationships. However, the piece reflects some new exploration of dyeing technique: a deliberate "mottling" of
the color within controlled gradations, achieving a
more organic effect.

Nancy Herman
Merion, Pennsylvania
Poppies III
Satins and cottons pieced and appliqued. 60'' x 72''

"Poppies III" is the third work in a series designed around the Liberty print which appears on the outside of the piece. The colors are arranged in a sequence to enhance the red of the poppies and to make the red and green of the satin "sing."

Nan Trichler
Willits, California
Africa
Machine pieced from one continuous length (approximately five yards) of 7" wide handwoven fabric from Mali, Africa. Machine quilted. 42" x 42"

Working within the unique limitations of the 7" wide fabric, I kept the design concept simple, creating only two different blocks. The image is the result of the interplay of these two. It was a delightful puzzle.

Faye Anderson
Denver, Colorado
Astral Macaroni with Blueberry Vinaigrette
100 percent cotton and polished cotton; cotton batting; hand applique and reverse applique. 36" x 36"

While others have come to quilting from backgrounds in architecture or painting, mine was advertising design. All my work begins with black and white elements with the 'subjects' applied in bold billboard colors. "Astral Macaroni" is very much like a keyline assembly of a print ad in which each motif is affixed to a clear acetate overlay and stacked, each bringing its piece to the whole image.

Most Innovative Use of the Medium Award
Co-Recipient

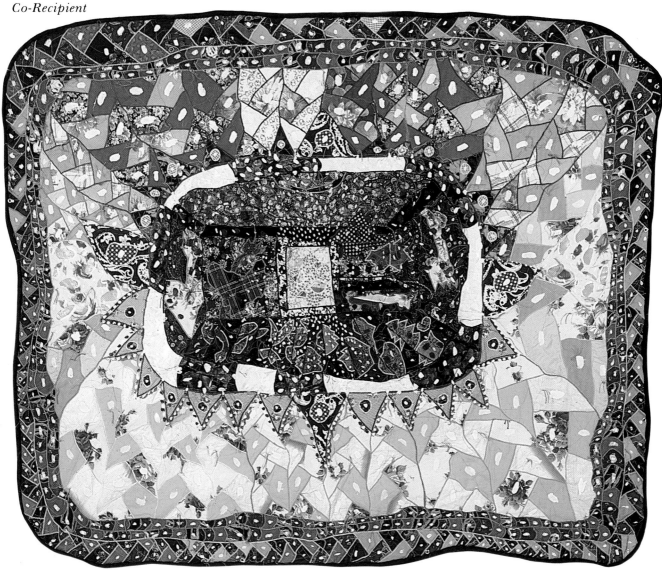

Therese May
San Jose, California
God Bless Us, One and All
Machine applique onto lightweight fabric; stuffed with batting; surface enhanced with areas of acrylic paint. 77" x 63"

The very center of this quilt contains a doorway through which we can see a Christmas tree enveloped in light. Outside of this we see a darkened room full of creatures and critters. Outside of this we see patches of pastel fabric which represent light again. These pastel patches are a large version of the braided rug pattern.

Most Innovative Use of the Medium Award
Co-Recipient

Therese May
San Jose, California
Sawblade
Machine applique onto canvas; surface enhanced with areas of acrylic paint. 78'' x 69''

The basic idea for this quilt came to me when I saw a giant sawblade at our local county fair. The blade had a wonderful landscape painted on it. In my sawblade, I used a braided rug pattern instead of a landscape. When I was working on this piece, I remember keeping track of how many pins I used (one for each patch), and it was a great number!

Linda MacDonald
Willits, California
Shooting Gallery
All cotton fabrics; machine pieced; hand appliqued and hand quilted. 82" x 92"

Shapes, fields, objects, and their juxtaposition within a unique environment are of interest to me. I have continued this pursuit within the confines of the traditionally-made quilt with much attention going to technique. The patterned back allows the quilting to be seen and enjoyed on its own, framed within a square block.

Nan Trichler
Willits, California
Tamiami Trail
Machine-pieced, hand-appliqued and hand-quilted cotton; polyester batting. 47" x 47"

Tamiami Trail is a highway in Florida that runs through the Everglades connecting Miami to Tampa. I grew up in this area. Although there was no conscious association with this place while I made the quilt, I recognized my nostalgia upon naming it.

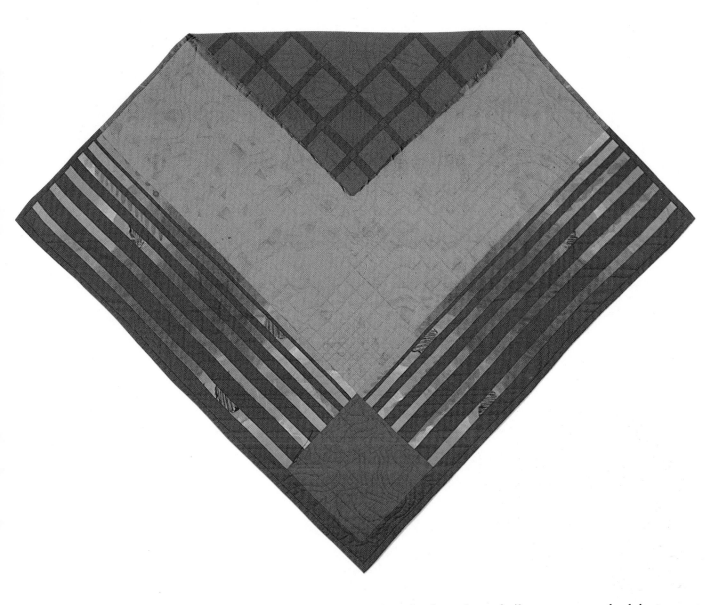

Judi Warren
Maumee, Ohio
Santa Fe: Sky Ceremony
Hand-dyed 100 percent cotton, hand painted and stenciled with createx textile pigment; machine strip-pieced and hand quilted. 48" x 37"

....a timeless place of silvery greens and adobe terra cotta embellished by the imagery of many cultures; where decorative patternings on Pueblo pottery are echoed in the soft geometry of gates and arches...reflected in the blue-violet sky; where architecture, nature and man are one—Santa Fe.

Invitational

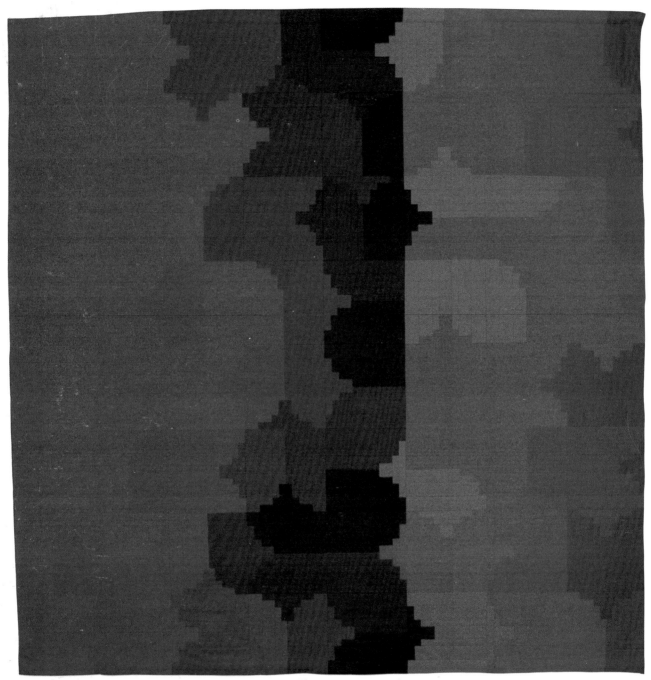

Photo provided by the artist.

Barbara Macey
Mt. Waverley, Victoria, Australia
Red Quilt
Cottons and synthetics; folded fabric strips are machine sewn to a base square and assembled. 71" x 71½"

By exploring ways of manipulating the basic "Log Cabin" block, I have discovered a surprisingly rich and flexible medium of expression. "Red Quilt" is a product of the imagination, an investigation of pattern using a single repeated unit, but mostly a celebration of bold form and vibrant color.

Ruth McDowell
Winchester, Massachusetts
Geraniums
Cottons and blends; machine pieced; hand appliqued;
hand quilted. 65'' x 76½''

Invitational

"Geraniums" is the fourth of my wallhangings based
on Penrose tiles (*Scientific American*, January 1977).
Penrose tiles, in addition to their other fascinating
properties, can be "inflated" and "deflated" and still fit
together. In this case, the flowers of the geraniums are
areas of deflation, made up of smaller versions of the
same tiles that form the rest of the quilt.

Suzanna Frosch
Narberth, Pennsylvania
Helenic Heritage I, II, and III
Cotton fabric; photo silk screen; plastic
stir sticks. 84" x 80"

In my studies I was shown an appliqued
quilt of coffee cups and saucers whose
imagery and grid format displayed a
wonderful sense of humor. I decided to
pay homage to this quilter by updating
her idea to fit the fast-paced 20th century.

Linda Karel Sage
Morgantown, Indiana
A Floosier Hoosier
New and recycled cottons and blends,
glazed chintz and antique fabrics; cotton
batting; machine pieced; hand quilted.
58" x 62"

I have been using needlework, quilts,
tramp art, unsigned home art and "out-
sider" art as inspiration for the wooden
constructions that I make. In looking for
these objects, I have had the good fortune
to meet a number of exceptional people
involved in quilting who have encouraged me to add quilting to my working
vocabulary.

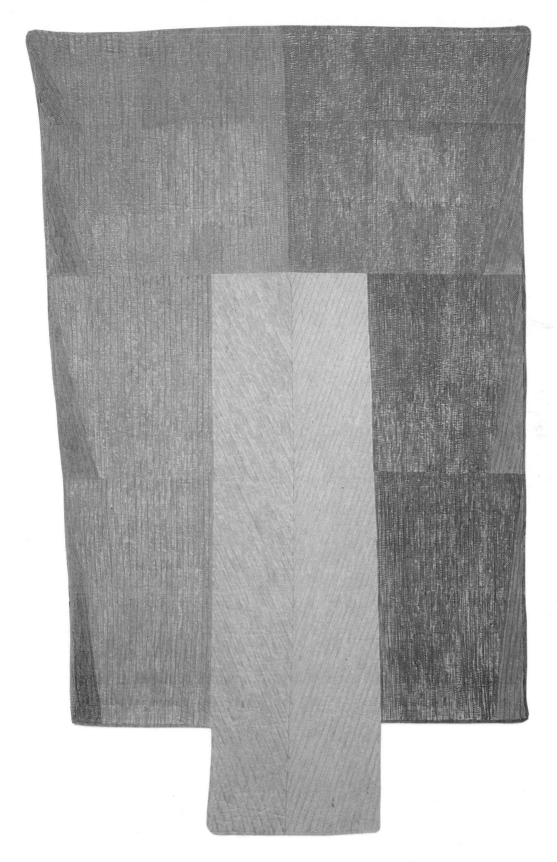

David Hornung
Saratoga Springs, New York
The Nile
Pieced cotton; hand quilted and hand dyed. 50'' x 83''

Invitational

I wanted to make a piece whose every aspect carried expressive weight. The construction has an unconventional shape that calls attention to its outline. The quilted lines are drawn freehand to lend them character. The dye was applied in layers of transparent wash with a small brush. This shows the mark of the hand that colored it.

Linda Levin
Wayland, Massachusetts
A Clear Day and No Memories
This quilt incorporates many procion-dyed fabrics as well as the marvelous paint rags of a talented friend. 62'' x 44''

For me, the tactile and visual qualities of different fabrics and the juxtaposition of colors and patterns provide endless possibilities for exploration. Although my work is in a sense pictorial, I try to capture not a specific, literal scene, but an atmosphere, a mood, or a moment.

Domini McCarthy Award for Exceptional Craftsmanship

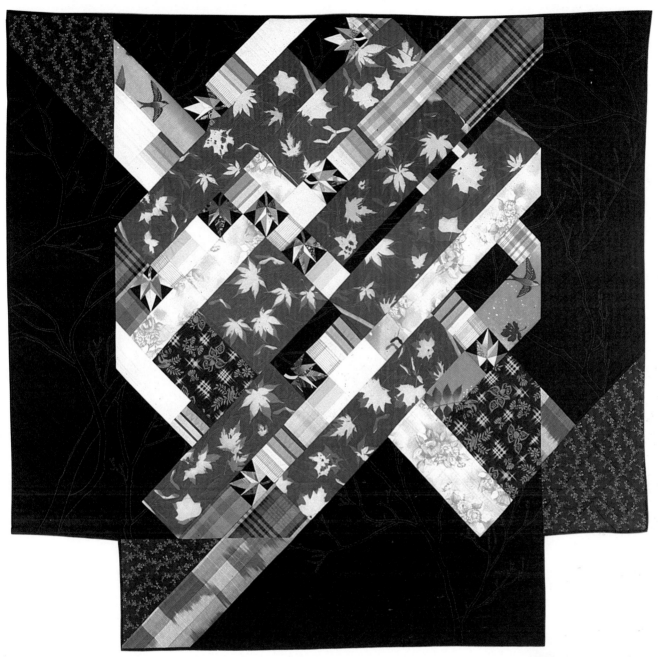

Nancy Halpern
Natick, Massachusetts
Maple Leaf Rag
Cotton and blends; cyanotype; hand and machine pieced; appliqued; hand quilted. 74'' x 71''

Begun as a winter jacket (the cyanotype strips were cuffs and facings, the maple leaves designed to drift across the dark blue background), this evolved into a Japanese four-poster futon quilt—a cross-cultural blend of New England bedquilt with the strong diagonals and presence of a Japanese kimono.

Detail

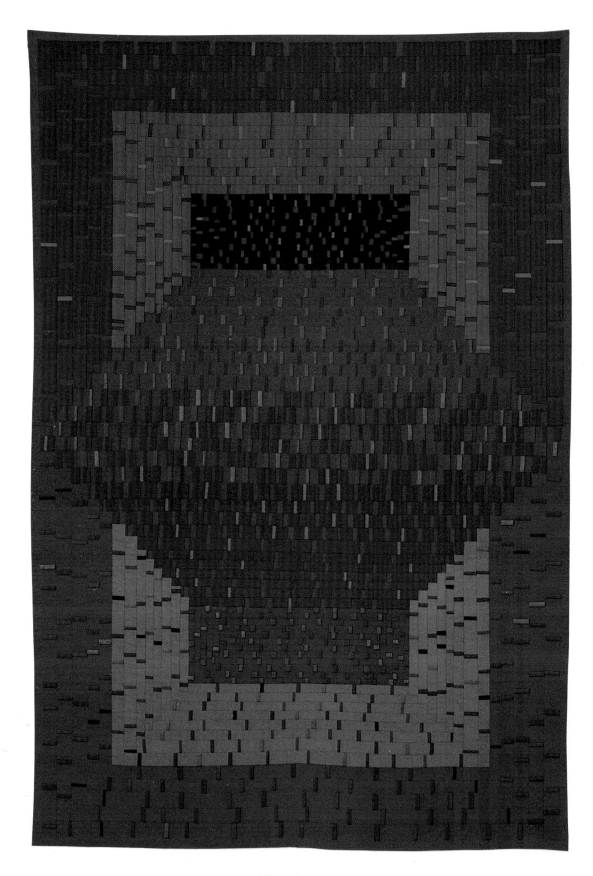

Judith Larzelere
Newbury, Massachusetts
Red and Blue Jar
100 percent cotton top is strip-pieced, recut into strips and then stitched onto batting and backing in one operation. 42'' x 62''

The subjects of this quilt are color interaction and the strip process by which it was constructed. A jar or basket form emerged as I worked and unexpectedly dominated the quilt. Colors that seem solid at a distance dissolve into vibrating flecks when viewed closely, and I like this change.

Deborah J. Felix
Rochester, New York
Prisoner of the Garden
Cotton; hand sewn; reverse applique and applique. 41" x 74"

I try to create a tension between my subjects and their environments, while at the same time looking at the absurdity of the situation. Using common subjects, such as a woman gardening, I take them one step further into abstraction through the use of intense colors and fabrics.

Pat Joyal
Duluth, Minnesota
Fredrique
Cotton/polyester fabrics machine pieced by the Seminole patchwork or strippiecing method; hand quilted by members of the North Country Quilters. 66" x 54"
Copyright 1983.

My husband's grandmother, Elizabeth Cartier, was one of the many anonymous women quilters who spent their lives making quilts. My work for the past ten years in surface design (batik, screen printing) has been primarily concerned with color and pattern, and seeing her quilts and blocks gave me inspiration to pursue quilting.

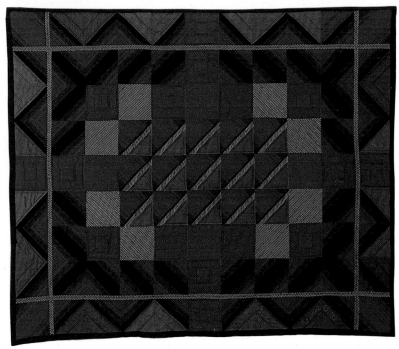

Soizik Labbens
Paris, France
Oh! Happy Days!
Solid cottons and chintzes; machine pieced; hand quilted. 53'' x 53''

My work is quite innovative. Color comes first: it's everywhere—nature, faces, garments, buildings—color is life and motion. I love to try all kinds of fabrics. Waiting for my plane at Kennedy Airport—a bit sad to leave all my friends, instructors and first American students, but my eyes full of happy "souvenirs"—I planned this quilt which reflected my feelings at the moment.

Ann Rhode
Berkeley, California
Basket Bazaar
Machine-pieced and appliqued cotton; polyester batting; hand quilted. 50½'' x 50½''

"Basket Bazaar" uses a traditional basket pattern which I wanted to give a contemporary feeling by the way I set the blocks and by the gradation of color in the background.

Jean Hewes
Fort Worth, Texas
Rocketing
Silk, cotton, rayon; machine pieced; machine appliqued. 92" x 74"

I am interested in the idea of veiling—the veiling of faces and body parts, the veiling of harsh colors to create illusions of depth, translucencies, blending, and floating abstractions.

Peggy Spaeth
Cleveland Heights, Ohio
Foldings III
100 percent cotton dyed by the artist; hand pieced by the artist; hand quilted by Maggie Kusner. 54" x 54" Copyright 1984.

(Collection of Mr. and Mrs. Daniel Costello)

Kathy Hall McKeever
Des Moines, Iowa
T.R.I.X.
Direct application of textile pigments on cotton and cheesecloth; embroidered and hand quilted. 31'' x 37''

By using squeeze bottles and sponges to draw and paint on the fabric, I attempt to create atmospheres of emotion using geometric imagery. "T.R.I.X." deals with trying to control and manipulate the various aspects of life.

Detail

Detail

Elaine O'Neil
Dorchester, Massachusetts
Memory Garden
Cyanotype (blueprinting) on cotton.
62½'' x 80''

My work in photography has often involved collage and montage. When I lived in Ohio, I became interested in quilting. About the same time I found out about emulsions that would enable me to print photographs on cloth, and I found that patchwork was the most natural way for me to work on a large scale.

JoAnn Giordano
Lafayette, Indiana
Ideal Love Mate Shrines
Screen print on cotton; color xerox transfer; hand and
machine quilting. 46'' x 39''

My postcard collection, particularly some 1940s ''Ideal
Love Mate'' cards, was the source of inspiration for this
quilt, a spoof on romantic love. I combined silkscreen
images from oriental rugs, Victoriana, 1950s magazines
and a scientific photograph with color xerox transfers
of postcards.

Terrie Hancock Mangat
Cincinnati, Ohio
Lightning Runner
Cottons and cotton blends; embroidery; straight seam machine piecing; cut-throughs and reverse applique.
65'' x 82''

The strength of this quilt lies in the attention to detail of the shapes of the children and the energy created by the lightning thrusts and intense color. This energy is further enhanced by the linear and circular quilting.

Invitational

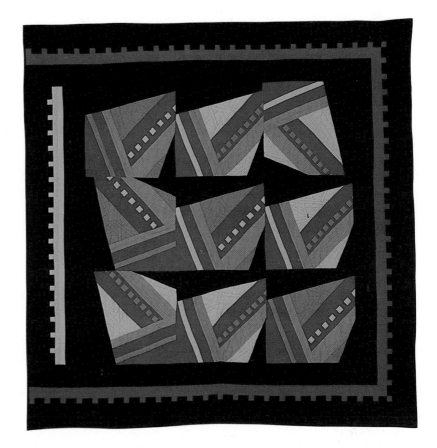

Jan Taylor Taskey
Vancouver, Washington
Red Alert
Machine-pieced, hand-quilted, strip-pieced cotton; cotton/polyester batting. 35" x 35"

This quilt was designed to achieve optical illusion using strip-piecing and bold colors to bring about an intense feeling. I carried the presence of optical illusion into the quilting of the background by creating an interwoven pattern.

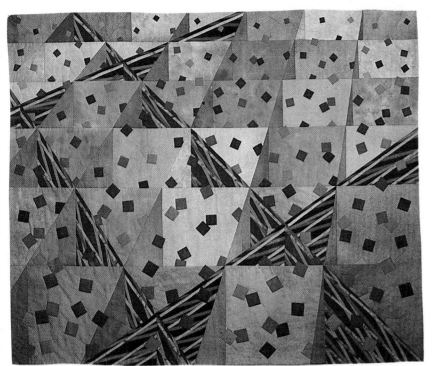

Photo provided by the artist.

Chris Wolf Edmonds
Lawrence, Kansas
Partitions II
Hand-painted and commercially-dyed cotton fabrics; machine pieced and quilted; hand appliqued. 65" x 54"

I continue to be intrigued with the illusion of light, space, and motion in the quilt design surface, and the construction challenge of perspective-drawn forms.

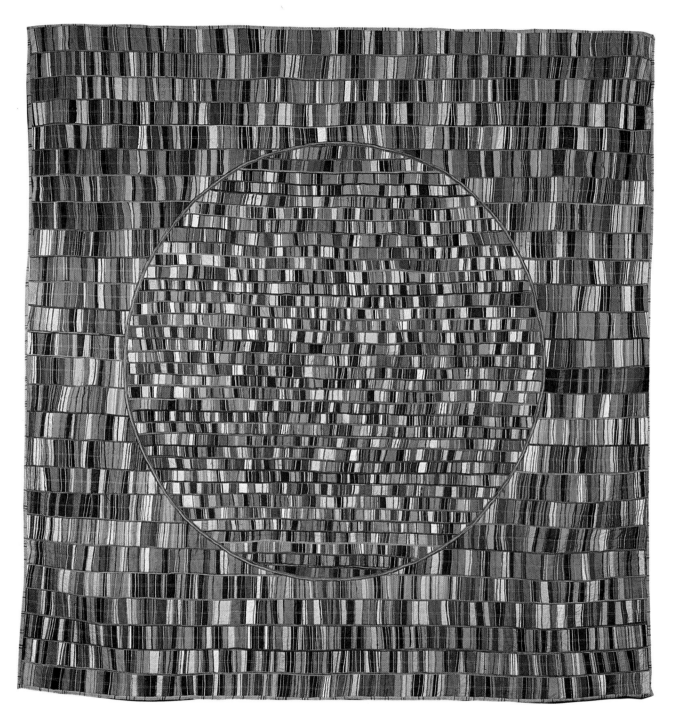

Lucy Wallis
Merriott, Somerset, England
Circle on Square I

Taffeta, overlaid with wool stitching; man-made interfill; cotton backed and tied; bound with velvet.
108'' x 108''

Jane Blair
Conshohocken, Pennsylvania
Parcheesi
Cotton and cotton/polyester fabric; polyester batting;
hand and machine pieced; machine quilted. 37'' x 37''

My aim is to make traditional patterns look fresh and
new. In this case variations of ''Pineapple'' and ''Log
Cabin'' were combined to form the design. From there
the choice of color and fabric was built piece by piece
on a work wall before construction.

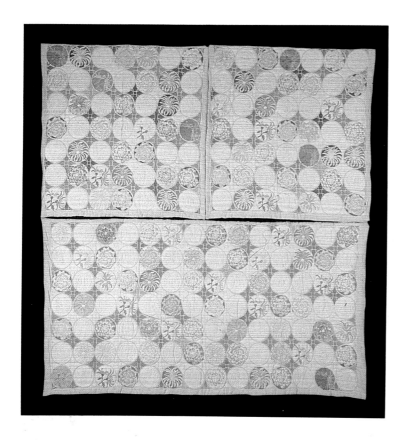

Marion Melody
Riverview, Michigan
Rondo of Life
Silk screen and batik on striped raw silk; hand painted Thai silk lining; hand quilted with silk twist. 72'' x 72''

I enjoy working with images that are reminiscent of our past. These recurring circles, some void and others sprinkled with flowers, are bridged with arcs. These stitched lines are threads of our existence connecting with joyous events and quiet times of reflection in our lives.

Rita DeWitt
Roswell, New Mexico
Too Many Airbrushed Smiles
Xerox 6500 Color Copier images heat-transferred to pima cotton; machine pieced; hand embroidery; no batting. 96'' x 81''

My recent work has involved examining those things about women in our culture that generally go unquestioned. These smiling heads were hairnet displays. I now recognize the fixed smiles on beauty queens, fashion models, women in cigarette ads. I wish I could find heads with that fashionable advertising pout!

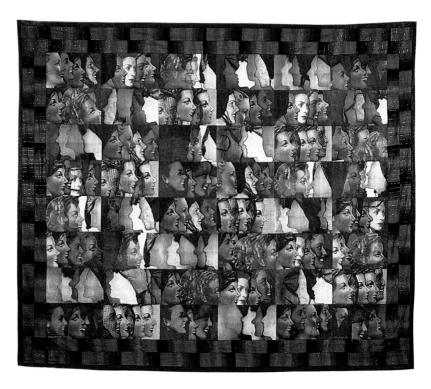

Photo provided by the artist.

Machiko Miyatani
Nishinomiya City, Hygo, Japan
Fantasy I
Cotton; machine pieced and hand quilted. 44'' x 54''

Miriam Nathan-Roberts
Berkeley, California
Lattice Interweave
Cottons and cotton blends; machine pieced; hand quilted by Sarah Hershberger of Charm, Ohio, under the direction of the artist. 80'' x 80''

My aim in this quilt was to achieve a sense of three-dimensionality on a flat surface. I also wanted a contrast between the strong design element, devoid of color, against a background of color to make the grid appear to float in front. It looks to me like woven steel.

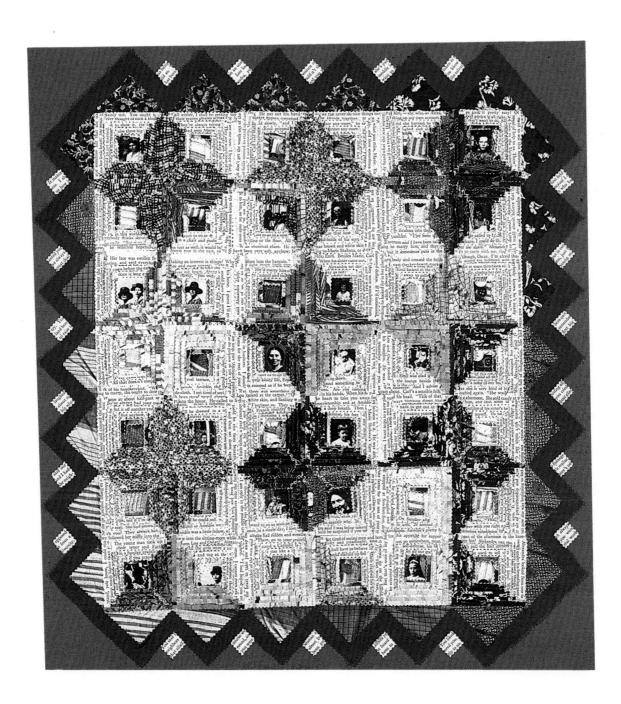

Christine Campbell
Charlotte, North Carolina
Chapter IX, The Pioneer Women, from
Willa Cather's **My Antonia**
Xerox, pinked and sewn paper. 40'' x 45''

I try to combine the things that I am interested in: American writers such as Willa Cather, Edna Ferber, and Mark Twain; office machines for copying and making multiples; pattern; images of women (from my postcard collection); and the notion that patterning by women of the past (and present) is Art.

Detail

Marilyn Stothers
Winnipeg, Manitoba, Canada
Curving Cubes
Cotton, polyester/cotton fabrics; machine pieced by curved strip-piecing and other methods; hand quilted and machine quilted; hand finished. 53" x 55"

I like to paint with fabric, and so I developed a fabric piecing method that I call "curved strip-piecing." The fascinating dimensional illusions of the cube challenged me to use "curved strip-piecing" in a cascading stream of colors flowing over these cubes, weaving in and out, reflecting in different light sources—like the paths of life.

Sue Alvarez
Charlotte, North Carolina
Tennessee Ribbons
Machine-pieced and appliqued ribbons of 100 percent cotton; cotton batting; machine quilted in concentric circles with touches of hand quilting. 60" x 55"

The variety of wide and thin ribbons of color reaching out beyond the limits of their quilt blocks are a remembrance for me of the women I met in Tennessee. The yellow ribbon tries to gather the colors together: to humor, encircle, and touch all the colors before moving upward and out. I am the yellow ribbon.

Janet Page-Kessler
New York, New York
Windmills of My Mind
Cotton and cotton blends; machine pieced and machine quilted. 41" x 45"

This piece is a statement about myself—an iconography of my mind and spirit using the symbolic colors of Christian art.

Margaret J. Miller
San Marcos, California
Melon Patch
Cotton and polyester/cotton blend fabrics; strip-pieced
by machine and hand quilted. 55" x 55"

The excitement of doing this series is putting strips of fabric colors that "feel right" together at random and discovering what happens in various block formats. The most delightful quilts for me (in process and in final product) have evolved from the simplest blocks: in this case, the square divided corner to corner.

Nancy Crow
Baltimore, Ohio
Passion III
Strip-pieced and pieced cottons and cotton blends;
hand quilted by Mrs. Eli M. Troyer. 85" x 85"

My most intense interest lies in the exploration of unusual color relationships based on a combination of emotional/intellectual attitudes influenced by the tension of living in solitude on a farm while at times craving intensely human stimulation. I am particularly interested in the ideas of Courage, Resilience, Self-Discipline, Drive, Intensity, Passion, Compassion, and the Production of a Body of Work despite great obstacles, be they physical or mental or both.

Lynne Ross
Greensboro, North Carolina
Seasons Series: Spring Lilies
Machine-pieced cottons and blends; hand
quilted. 48" x 48"

"Spring Lilies" is the most recent quilt in
my Seasons Series—and my personal favor-
ite. Working in a series was a great expe-
rience for me and allowed me to develop a
design to a higher degree than I've
achieved before. I recommend it to every
serious artist.

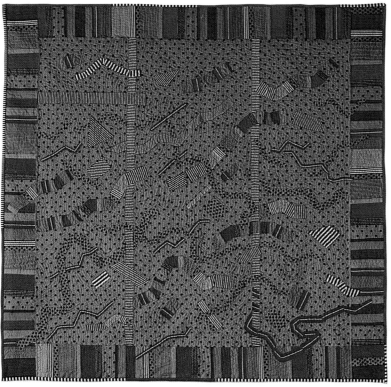

Margot Strand Jensen
Aurora, Colorado
Coming Unglued
Hand appliqued; machine pieced; free-
form machine quilted with metallic
thread. 53½" x 51"

"Coming Unglued" is a statement about
sanity and how the mind begins to frag-
ment when disruption occurs. The verti-
cal bars symbolize the restraints one puts
on one's life—*i.e.*, prisons of the mind.
The pink curlique symbolizes the final
unraveling of the mind—the "coming
unglued."

Photo provided by the artist.

Miriam Nathan-Roberts
Berkeley, California
Nancy's Fancy
Cotton and cotton blends; machine pieced; hand quilted
by Sarah Hershberger of Charm, Ohio, and by Miriam
Nathan-Roberts. 54'' x 54''

In working with illusions of depth, I decided to do
boxes that slowly disintegrate. I kept three—lower left
center. The others have one or more sides blown out.
My fellow quilt artist Nancy Halpern convinced me to
change a serious study to a whimsical one by using the
unusual fabrics I love.

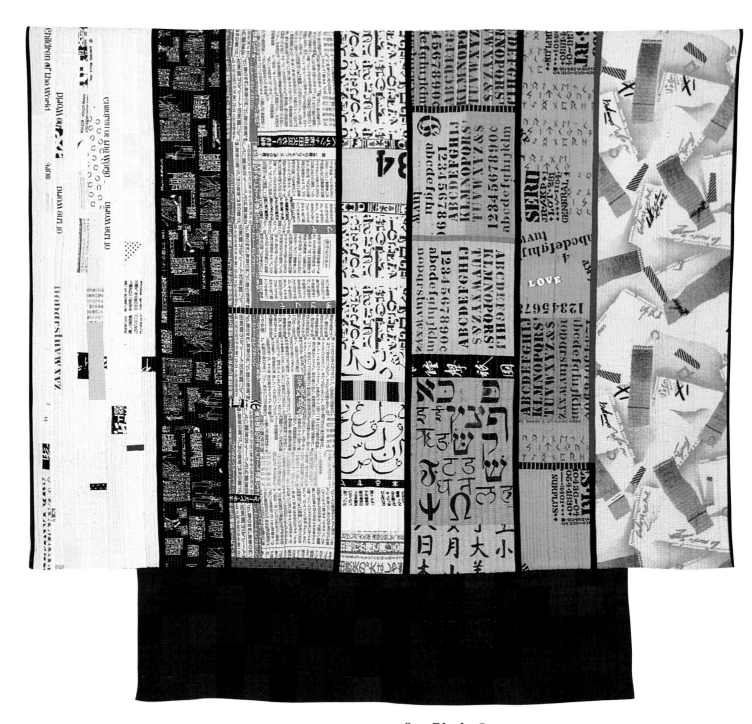

Sara Rhodes-Long
Ft. Bragg, California
Understanding Each Other
Cottons and cotton blends; some hand stenciling; polyester batting; buttons; braille alphabet. 53" x 49"

To the wonder and beauty of alphabets and markings.

Lori Barraco Smith
Sand Lake, New York
Brugh Na Boinne
Hand-dyed cotton; machine appliqued and machine quilted; stretched on a frame. 26½" x 34¼"

For two years I have been haunted by Jean McMann's photographs in her book *Riddles of the Stone Age* (Thames and Hudson). They depict the massive stone chambers constructed by neolithic man to capture the sun's light at solstice. I have attempted to abstract the essence of winter light as it illuminates the chamber. Brugh Na Boinne is the ancient Irish name for this particular stone construction.

Radka Donnell
Zurich, Switzerland
The Plumage of the Ascending Goddess
Cottons and blends hand and machine pieced by Radka Donnell; machine quilted by Claire Mielke. 70" x 90"

A sense of rebirth and being helped to a higher level of self was the guiding impulse of this work. I started at the edges and moved in and up, pulling myself out of every kind of rut and low.

Photo provided by the artist.

Julie Berner
Eugene, Oregon
One Fine Day
Machine patchwork in cotton; hand quilted by Thekla Schnitker. 40" x 40"

I am continually inspired by organization and color in nature and the environment. I build my own patterns of progressive shapes with pencil on a geometric grid. When a composition is finished, I match the colors of fabrics with gouache to add depth, movement and intensity to the design.

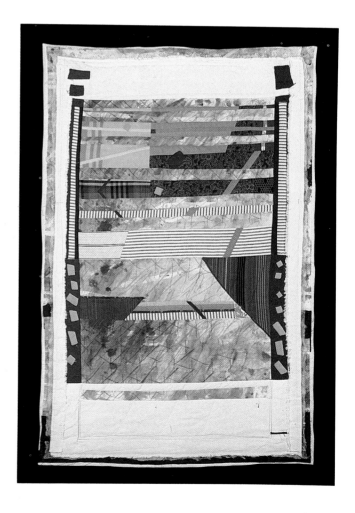

Elizabeth A. Busch
Bangor, Maine
Haystack Sunrise
Procion-dyed cotton; oil crayon; canvas machine and hand pieced; appliqued; hand quilted. 41" x 60"

The coast of Maine and Haystack Mountain School of Crafts in Deer Isle, Maine, are energy, are inspiration, are creativity, are excitement, are vitality, are "Haystack Sunrise."

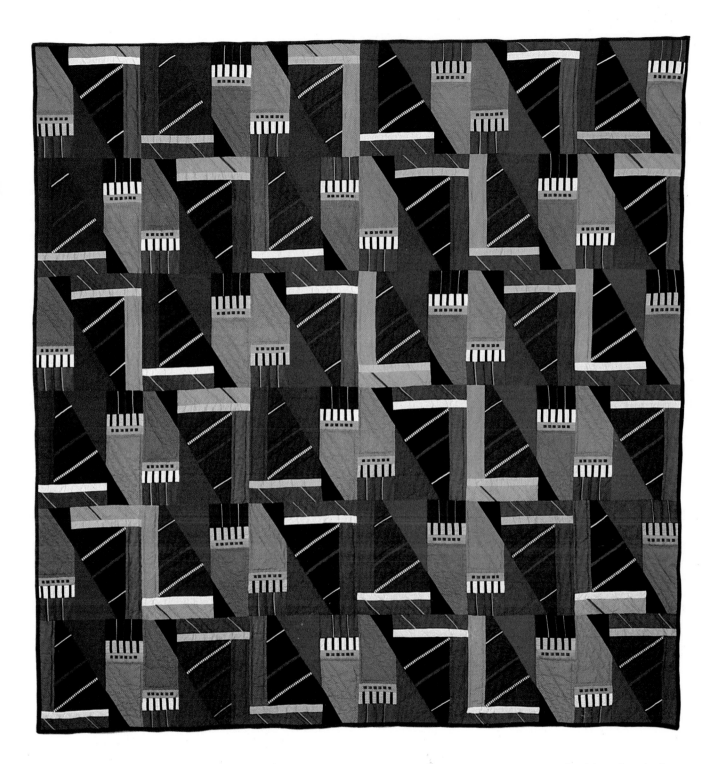

Sharon Heidingsfelder
Little Rock, Arkansas
Melody in Color
100 percent cotton fabric; strip-piecing combined with traditional piecing, hand quilted by Mrs. Abe Troyer, Millersburg, Ohio. 70" x 70"

This is the first time I've worked with strip-piecing. Actually, this is the very first quilt I have made. My husband, who is a musician, named the quilt for the section of it that looks like piano keys.

Margot Strand Jensen
Aurora, Colorado
Harlequinade
Machine pieced and hand appliqued; machine quilted
with metallic thread. 57½'' x 45''

"Harlequinade" is a whimsical piece depicting fantasy
as well as its dictionary definition: that part of a play or
pantomine in which the Harlequin (comic character in
spangled and diamond patterned tights) plays mis-
chievous parts; comic pranks, buffoonery.

Risë Nagin
Pittsburgh, Pennsylvania
Tunnel Vision: Henri Matisse at Blue Mountain
Cotton, silk, polyester; applique; embroidery. 47" x 50"

"Tunnel Vision: Henri Matisse at Blue Mountain" takes its motif from the Pennsylvania Turnpike. I wanted to put the overlooked objects on the road and its surrounding landscape (in this case the Blue Mountain Tunnel) into the context of the Japanese kimono with its connotations of poetic beauty.

Photo provided by the artist.

Photo provided by the artist.

Claire Starr
Washington, D.C.
In Celebration
Cotton and cotton blend fabrics; metallic and silk thread; hand-stitched and hand sewn. 21" x 18"

My work has been influenced by a recent rekindling of an interest in astronomy. I have attempted to set up a tension between color, line and shapes such that each is essential to maintain the equilibrium of the whole.

Pamela G. Johnson
Kansas City, Missouri
Yellow Square II
Hand-quilted, machine-pieced cotton; polyester batting. 48¾" x 48¾" Copyright 1984.

The pieced structure of this work is based on an antique quilt composed of alternating light and dark triangles (value contrast). I set out to expand on that design's limited notion of contrast and to explore additional ways in which color can be manipulated within this simple format.

STATEMENT OF
DAIRY BARN EXECUTIVE DIRECTOR

The Dairy Barn Southeastern Ohio Cultural Arts Center is proud to produce the fourth biennial *Quilt National* and proud, too, of having played a major part in promoting the growth and acceptance of the quilt as an art form. In 1979 when the first *Quilt National* was organized, it was the only juried contemporary quilt exhibition in the United States. Since then, we have been pleased to see other juried contemporary quilt competitions come into existence, proof of the vitality of this art form and its appeal to artists and viewers alike.

The 1985 exhibit maintains *Quilt National's* claim to be the leading showcase for the contemporary quilt. American artists from 44 states and artists from eight other nations submitted more than 900 works for consideration, and the jurors' decisions resulted in an exciting group of 73 works representing 27 states and six other nations. The exhibit also includes 10 invitational pieces by major quilt artists.

A major national exhibition is made possible by the hard work, skills and financial support of hundreds of individuals. The Dairy Barn would especially like to thank Hilary Fletcher for her dedication in coordinating both the 1983 and the 1985 *Quilt National* exhibits—a task somewhat akin to creating a fine quilt. Special appreciation is also due to Best Products Foundation, Fairfield Processing Corporation, the Ohio Arts Council and the State of Ohio's Opportunities for the Arts Program for their vital support.

Finally, we would like to thank the quilt artists, who continue to surprise, delight and inform us as they expand the art of the quilt and share their explorations and discoveries in exhibits such as *Quilt National.*

Pamela S. Parker, Executive Director
The Dairy Barn
Southeastern Ohio Cultural Arts Center

COORDINATOR'S STATEMENT

When the first *Quilt National* opened in 1979, viewers were startled by what they saw. The boldly colored geometrics, the abstracts, and even the representational pieces were overpowering. It was obvious that many of these pieces were not intended to cover beds—therefore, they were not quilts! Faced with the unexpected, many viewers of *Quilt National '79* concentrated on the technical elements in a work and ignored the overall image.

Just as *Quilt National* has changed over the years, so have the visitors who now travel from many parts of the globe to see it. While today's viewers still expect careful workmanship, they are also excited and intrigued by the nature of the images and the seemingly endless variety of materials and techniques used to create them.

From its inception, *Quilt National* has had as its purpose the promotion of contemporary quilting as an art form. Seeing the overwhelming vitality and strength of the *Quilt National '85* entries, and the acceptance and understanding of them displayed by exhibition visitors, I believe that purpose has been achieved.

Hilary M. Fletcher
Quilt National '85
Coordinator

The Dairy Barn Southeastern Ohio Cultural Arts Center, Athens, Ohio.

Quilt National '79 Installation.

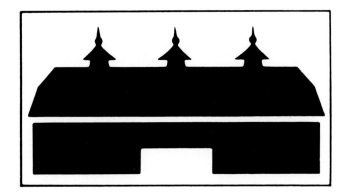

THE DAIRY BARN

THE DAIRY BARN

The Dairy Barn Southeastern Ohio Cultural Arts Center has gained national recognition as a showplace for the finest in traditional and contemporary arts and crafts.

A classic example of barn architecture of the 19th and early 20th century, the Dairy Barn was built in 1914 on the grounds of the Athens Mental Health Center. For many years it housed prize Holstein cattle as part of the center's farm-based activity therapy program.

In 1977, when the State of Ohio announced plans to raze the building, area citizens rallied to save it. Their efforts began the Barn's transformation into an art center for Southeast Ohio, a region whose rural beauty has long attracted—and continues to attract—artists and craftspeople.

Set in the rolling Appalachian foothills, the Dairy Barn is an impressive 200-foot long structure that includes 7,000 square feet of exhibition space. In 1978 it was named to the National Register of Historic Places. As funding becomes available, it is undergoing a carefully planned process of renovation. Most recently, the Barn received title to 32 surrounding acres, thus assuring that its rare setting would remain unspoiled.

The Dairy Barn is organized as a non-profit corporation, and its many programs and exhibitions depend on the efforts and expertise of hundreds of volunteers. Financial support comes from memberships, admission fees, corporate and individual contributions and government and private grants.

With its vast slate roof, three cupolas, hooded dormers, 27 windows and red brick paving, the Dairy Barn is a unique setting for exhibitions and events as varied and colorful as Quilt National, the Hallmark National Jigsaw Puzzle Championships and the American Contemporary Works in Wood exhibit.

Quilt National '81 Installation.

Quilt National '83 Installations.

INDEX